This book belongs to :

BELIEVE.
PERSIST.
ACHIEVE

Dream
big, act
now

STRIVE
FOR
EXCELL
ENCE

Dream it, be it

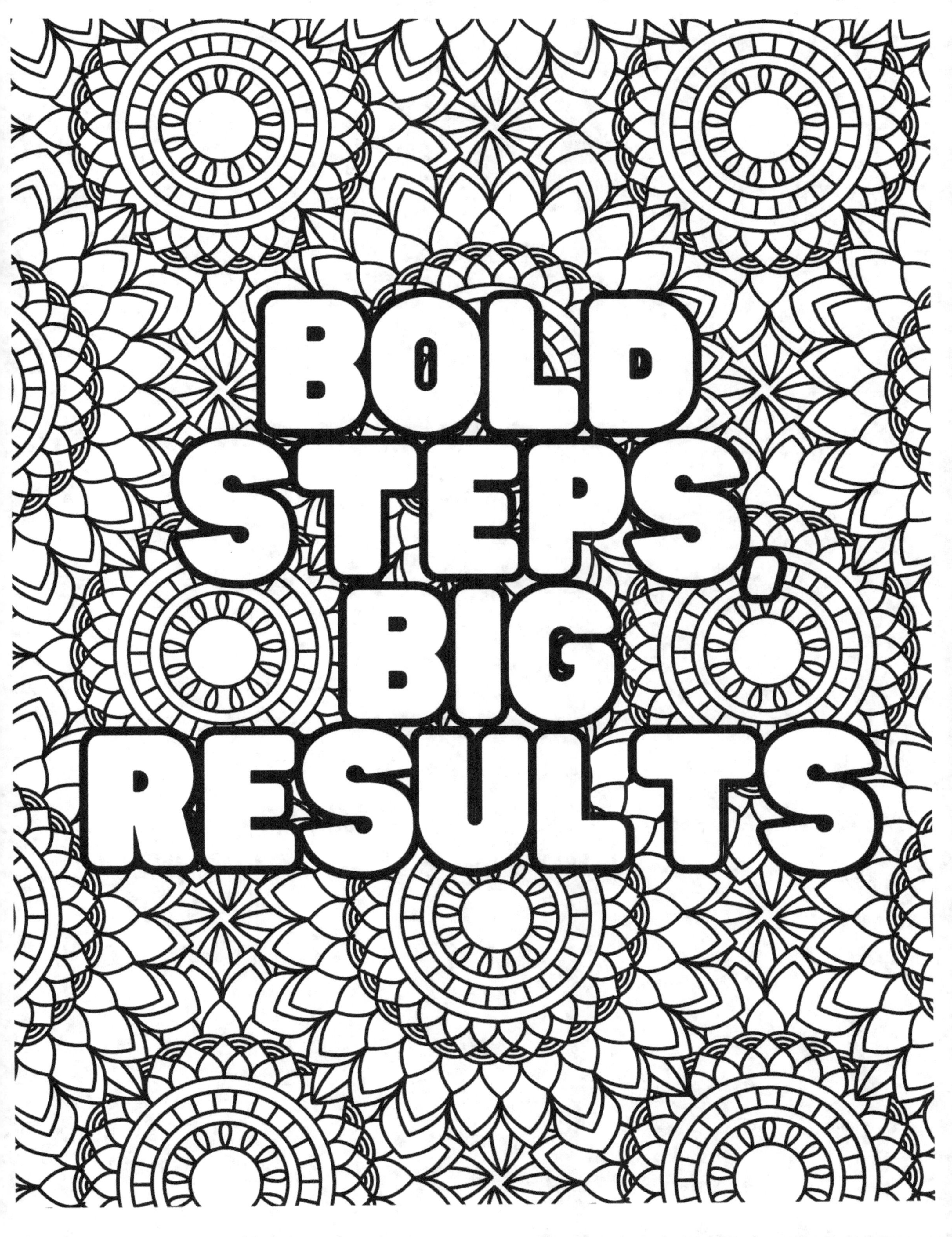

BOLD STEPS, BIG RESULTS

STRIVE FOR YOUR BEST.

WORK
HARD,
DREAM
BIGGER

BOLD
ACTIONS,
BIG
RESULTS'

CHASE
DREAMS
RELENTL
ESSLY

CHASE
DREAMS
RELENTL
ESSLY

CREATE
BELIEVE
ACHIEVE

Dream,
hustle,
achieve

STAY
FOCUSED.
STAY
DETERMINED

SUCCESS:
EARN IT

Bold moves, big outcomes

BELIEVE,
ACHIEVE,
INSPIRE

Stay
hungry
stay
foolish

Determin
ationfuels
success

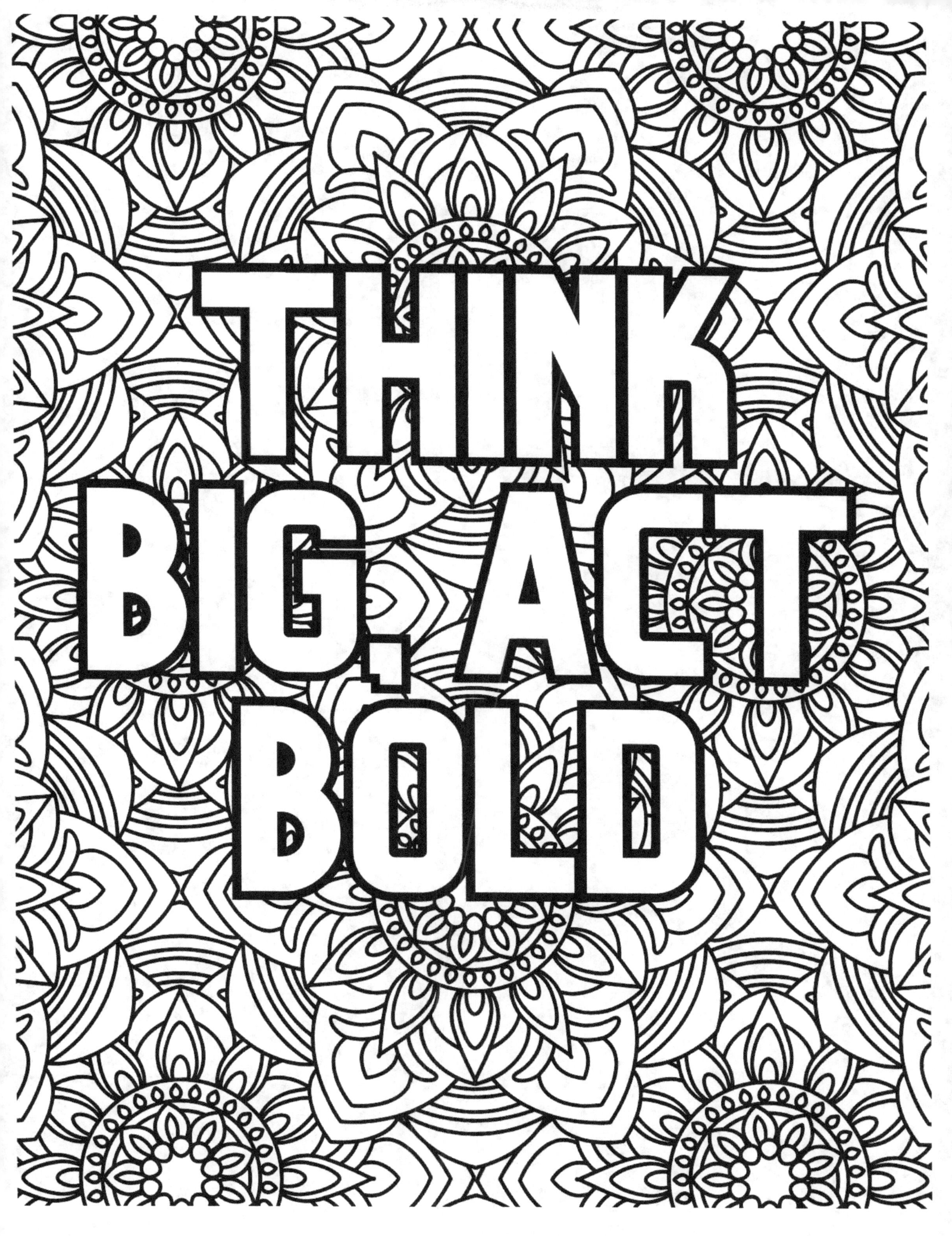

THINK
BIG, ACT
BOLD

START,
ENDURE,
FINISH

EMBRACE
THE
JOURNEY

WORK HARD,
DREAM BIG

DREAM
IT,
ACHIEVE
IT

Bold
action, big
results

STRIVE,
CONQUER,
REPEAT.

Bold
Steps, Big
Results

Fear
less, do
more

CREATE,
CONQUER,
CELEBRATE

CHASE
GOALS, NOT
APPLAUSE

THRIVE IN
EVERY
CHALLENGE

RISE
AFTER
EVERY
FALL

Work
smart
dreambig

FOCUS.
COMMIT.
CONQUER.

PASSION
DRIVES
PERSEVE
RANCE

INSPIRE.
LEAD.
SUCCEED

Bold dreams, brave heart

SEIZE
EVERY
OPPORT
UNITY

BELIEVE.
ACHIEVE.
OVERCOME

Act
boldly,
succeed
brilliantly

STRIVE,
THRIVE,
NEVER
SETTLE.

PUSH LIMITS,
ACHIEVE
GREATNESS

RISE
ABOVE
CONQUER
ALL

Success
no
Shortcuts

WORK
HARD
STAY
HUMBLE

Dream,
believe,
achieve

BELIEVE,
CONQUER,
THRIVE

CREATE
YOUR
SUNSHINE

Dream
plan
execute

Achieve,
believe,
succeed

DARE
GREATLY,
CONQUER
FEAR

DREAM
BIG,
HUSTLE
HARD.